THE CATECHISM OF THE CATHOLIC CHURCH:
Familystyle

We Pray

VOLUME 4

David M. Thomas, Ph.D.
& Mary Joyce Calnan

ThomasMore®
A DIVISION OF TABOR PUBLISHING
Allen, Texas

NIHIL OBSTAT
Reverend Edward L. Maginnis, S.J.
Censor Deputatus

IMPRIMATUR
Very Rev. Donald F. Dunn
Vicar General for the Diocese
    of Colorado Springs

October 5, 1994

The nihil obstat and imprimatur are official declarations that a book or pamphlet is free of doctrinal or moral error. No implication is contained therein that those have granted the nihil obstat and the imprimatur agree with the content, opinion, or statements expressed.

ACKNOWLEDGMENTS

Scripture quotations are taken from or adapted from the Good News Bible text, Today's English Version. Copyright © American Bible Society 1966, 1971, 1976, 1993.

Excerpts from the English translation of the *Catechism of the Catholic Church for the United States of America,* copyright © 1994, United States Catholic Conference, Inc.—Liberia Editrice Vaticana.

DESIGN: Davidson Design

Send all inquiries to:
Thomas More Publishing
200 East Bethany Drive
Allen, Texas 75002–3804

Printed in the United States of America

ISBN 0–88347–298–8

2 3 4 5 6   00 99 98 97 96

Contents

It is the tradition of families to hand down their most treasured possessions from one generation to the next. Each new generation accepts the special gift with great reverence, because it connects the family with its history, identity, values, and stories.

It is in this tradition that the family which is the Church has treasured the gift of faith and the inheritance that the Creator bestows on us as the children of God. The gift of faith has been treasured and preserved down through the ages in the stories of Scripture, the teachings of the Church, the writings of saints and scholars, the celebrations of sacramental life, and the witness of lives of love and service.

In this spirit, our Holy Father Pope John Paul II convoked an extraordinary assembly of the Synod of Bishops in 1985 which began the task of drafting a compendium of Catholic doctrine to insure that the inheritance of our faith story, values, and traditions would be accessible to and suited for the generations of the present and the future. The *Catechism of the Catholic Church* is primarily a resource of doctrinal, moral, social, and spiritual teaching for all those who have been given the responsibility of passing on our faith inheritance.

David Thomas and Mary Joyce Calnan have taken the *Catechism* down from the shelf, as it were, have given it life, and have made it an inheritance that will be passed down from family to family, from generation to generation. Their four-volume *Catechism of the Catholic Church: Familystyle* is the first local or national catechism written from the original resource. They are faithful and careful stewards of the Church's treasure of faith and values. First, they have divided their familystyle catechism into the same divisions as the *Catechism of the Catholic Church*—Creed, Sacraments,

Life in Christ, and Prayer. Second, the reader can follow the development of topics in the same order as the new *Catechism*. Third, they connect the doctrine of our faith to the reality of life today in a process and style that touches your heart and your spirit. By adapting the *Catechism* to the culture and lifestyle of the family, they "unwrap" the *Catechism* and allow us to know our God as intimately caring and as connected to our everyday lives.

David and Mary Joyce are exemplary disciples of the Master Teacher as they skillfully and sensitively tell extraordinary stories of ordinary people, which draw you into the Word of God in Scripture and into the particular teaching of our faith tradition. Each chapter invites the reader to reflect on story, Scripture, doctrine and then to apply this to his or her own life as a family member. Each chapter concludes with a prayer for the rich resource of Church tradition adapted to the language and life of the family. Although this resource is intended primarily for families in all the many shapes and forms of family systems today, I believe that *The Catechism of the Catholic Church: Familystyle* will be a special gift to everyone in catechetical, liturgical, and other pastoral ministries as a resource and as a spiritual companion.

I am deeply honored to be invited to write the foreword for this book. David Thomas and Mary Joyce Calnan have a rich background in family life ministry. Their *Catechism of the Catholic Church: Familystyle* reflects that ministry as this work brings faith to life and life to faith. I know that readers will join with me in expressing my deepest gratitude for this gift of faith and love that will undoubtedly become a new classic in American Catholic spirituality.

Howard J. Hubbard
Bishop of Albany, NY

Introduction

You have just opened *We Pray,* the fourth book in a four-volume series. This final volume builds on and completes the circle of the first three, *We Believe, We Celebrate,* and *We Love.* The four volumes of this familystyle catechism correspond to the four parts of the *Catechism of the Catholic Church* recently issued by the Vatican.

Pope John Paul II requested that the catechism of the whole Church be adapted to local churches. In *We Pray* we connect the life of the family with part four of the Vatican's catechism, "Christian Prayer."

Some say that this last part of the Vatican's catechism should have been placed at its beginning because it deals with such an important part of our faith, our life of prayer. In prayer, we connect with God. We listen to God and we express our response to God. Our prayer happens during times of joy and times of sadness, moments of need and moments of satisfaction, in good times and not so good times—just like family, because open and honest communication is the lifeblood of the family.

Communication connects us from our first heartbeat to our last. Words of love and concern draw us closer together. Words of indifference and hostility pull us apart. And sometimes silence totally blocks the flow of life between us.

All of this bears strong and direct similarities to our life of prayer. Perhaps the simplest description of prayer is "conversation with God." But as simple as conversation and communication may seem to be, in real life they are often quite challenging. The same can be true of prayer.

The prayer life of our Church is filled with family language. When Jesus addressed God in prayer, he used a word in his language that is close to our word *Dad.* Very familylike, very homey, very intimate. We are invited to do the same.

Let us begin.

CHAPTER ONE
Prayer—
Communication Godstyle

. . . when the Great Spirit was ready.

The day was hot, really hot. But somehow this didn't bother the people in the truck. Not today. For today was the day they waited for each year—the day of coming to the ancient burial grounds. On this holy day they celebrated their connection to the living and the dead, to the earth, and to their maker. This was a day of family.

They had only a short way yet to go. They used to go more often when they lived on the reservation, but now they made the journey just once a year, even though they lived only twenty miles or so away.

They were all a little sad. Not only because of the solemnity of the occasion, but because the oldest son, John (*Nighthawk* in their native tradition), had refused to come. As far back as the elders could remember, this had never happened before and was a surprising thing.

But John's not coming also angered the grown-ups, because they worried about the loss of their treasured traditions. However, they tried to concentrate on this and on the holiness of the ceremony they would celebrate together.

When they arrived, everybody knew exactly what to do and went about getting ready. About them glowed an aura of expectation, for they all knew that this ceremony brought each of them further on their own life's journey.

Once they had prepared their bodies and the ceremonial objects, they began. At first, the drums and intonations seemed to be softer than usual, and the elder motioned to his son to increase the intensity of the beat. Within minutes, the sacred experience engulfed all of them.

Ancient words and gestures called forth the cultural connection with their creator and sustainer. The movements, while unique to each person, seemed part of a choreographed whole as if they'd rehearsed each step and sound and gesture for only this moment.

Then the ceremony ceased, and they all turned to the sun. Sitting down to fully absorb the power of their feelings, the small gathering fell silent. Each rested, and each listened to his or her own heartbeat. Each waited for the holy reflection time to end. And it would, when the Great Spirit was ready.

Then they heard the car. Because the area was so remote, they were surprised that another car could be so near. And they felt some resentment as well for being distracted and invaded by non-Indian people.

They watched the dust, raised by the vehicle, swirl into the sky. Then they heard the car stop at the bottom of the hill, out of sight. All was quiet; their awareness of the Spirit was still present. The heart of the day permeating their centers.

Then they saw him. His head, and then the rest of his body, came over the rise out of the gully. His head hung down in shame and embarrassment.

All of them stood to face him. For a moment their presence was somber. And then his grandfather's face broke in an unashamed grin and he said, simply, "You are here."

"I am the vine, and you are the branches. Those who remain in me, and I in them, will bear much fruit; for you can do nothing without me. Those who do not remain in me are thrown out like a branch and dry up; such branches are gathered up and thrown into the fire, where they are burned. If you remain in me and my words remain in you, then you will ask for anything you wish, and you shall have it. My Father's glory is shown by your bearing much fruit; and in this way you become my disciples. I love you just as the Father loves me; remain in my love. If you obey my commands, you will remain in my love, just as I have obeyed my Father's commands and remain in his love."

John 15:5–9

To sense God, we need to be still within.

Jesus is sitting and talking with his friends at the supper table. Almost everything he says holds a deep meaning because this is the night before his death and he is probably aware of this. His apostles remain unaware.

Jesus is doing all he can do to finish teaching them; he is giving them a review, as teachers do, of what he has said and done and of what his words and actions have meant. He wants his followers to understand the importance of his life.

Perhaps Jesus is like the Native American elders in our opening story who want all their children to understand the importance and deeper meaning of what they say and do.

In this gospel passage, Jesus is telling us how important we are to God. Our relationship to this great God we love and worship is like a branch to a vine. Through Jesus, God invites us to live in this union, to stay connected—forever.

Jesus is teaching his friends and us about the importance of recognizing how we belong to God. We do this all the time in family. We show this belonging with comments such as "You have your mother's eyes" and "She loves to follow her daddy around" and "I felt so sad on Christmas because I missed my parents."

We're connected, and we need to communicate that to one another. (The greeting card and gift industry know that full well. They know how to get to us!) We let each other know what we're thinking and feeling in many, many ways. We're important to each other. We couldn't hurt each other so easily if we weren't.

This is obvious in the family in our opening story. They are important to each other, and they communicate their connectedness in several ways: (1) Together, they celebrate their long traditions, which connect them with their deceased family and tribe members, with the earth, and with God. (2) Together, they long for their missing young son to be there with them. (3) Together, they meditate on the connections they have just celebrated.

Patiently, God waits for us to connect. God is always there, connected to us. God longs to listen and to speak to us in hundreds of ways! And we? We must be aware of that connection, hold on to it, treasure it, cherish it. We must absorb the love that God offers us.

Reflecting on our God is one way to open ourselves to our connectedness. Reflecting invites us to quiet down inside so that we can meditate on the wonders of our God. To sense God, we need to be still within.

Conversation is at the heart of prayer.

Just as blood brings life to the body and nourishes it, so prayer brings the presence and love of our nourishing God to all the parts of our life. And, in a sense, prayer, like blood, also carries away the waste materials. Just like blood, prayer keep us healthy and alive!

The simplest (and perhaps the best) description of prayer is that it is conversation with God. Conversation is at the heart of prayer. God talks; we listen. We talk; God listens. And sometimes prayer becomes more than words. Just as two human beings can say no words, but can simply listen to one another's heart; so, in prayer, we can listen to the love in God's heart and God can listen to the love or pain or sorrow or grief or anger in ours. Even if we say nothing. That's what being present to us is all about.

In this small book, we will study prayer, which nourishes and ties together the various aspects of our life. The word we will use to describe our relationship to God and our communication with God is *spirituality*. Each of us possesses a spirituality because each of us has a relationship to God. In order to understand this better, let's take the word *spirituality* apart and reshape it. Here's what we get: *Spirit—into—reality*. If we say these three words quickly, they begin to sound like *spirituality*. Thus, our spirituality is the way each of us allows our relationship with God to enter our day-to-day life.

We're talking about the everyday, ordinary stuff of life! So our spirituality includes matters such as who is important in our lives, what we think and do about world hunger, how we relate to our next-door neighbor. Even matters such as what kind of a car we drive and where we drive it are part of our spirituality. All of these are ordinary aspects of life purposefully woven into our life with God.

Another way of getting in touch with our spirituality is to ask what our basic values are. What's really important to us? Some of our values are founded on genuine love of our neighbor; others may be rooted in fear. Some may serve simply to protect our stuff, our possessions, our property. Others are connected with our family.

Ordinary aspects of life . . . woven into our life with God.

We have all heard the phrase *family values.* But what do these words really mean? That my family comes first no matter what? That I believe that only one kind of family should exist? That I connect my experience of my family with my experience of God? There are many possibilities, and all come under the umbrella of "Spirit-into-reality"—spirituality.

Spirituality is the way we live each day; prayer is what connects each of these days with God. Without prayer, we risk the danger of becoming like an empty container, a hollow vessel. Or even worse, we risk the danger of appearing outwardly virtuous, while interiorly, we may be terribly self-centered and manipulative. Jesus used one of his most biting images to speak his horror of such hypocrites. He called them "whitewashed tombs" meaning that they looked all right on the outside (fresh white paint) but inside they were filled with rotting flesh. This powerful image is as important today as ever.

This small book of the familystyle catechism mirrors the fourth book of the *Catechism of the Catholic Church,* which is on Christian prayer. Why is prayer treated last? Is it the least important? No. On the contrary, it is the Church's way of reminding us that prayer is what connects our beliefs (the first book), our sacramental celebration (the second book), and our morality (the third book) with our lives. Prayer nourishes (gives life to) our faith, our celebrations, and our morality.

The same can be said for the life of the family. Communication and conversation among family members give life to our basic beliefs, our celebration and routines, and our lifestyle. Without family communication, our beliefs become private, we forget our celebrations, and each of us in the family lives a more or less independent lifestyle. Then we have no family life; we have only our own separate existences. Family conversation, family connecting, is the way we personally connect or knit our lives together—as family. It brings family *into* reality.

Connecting through conversation

All of us need and want to be connected, whether we admit this or not. We want to be connected to ourselves, to other people, and to God. But connectedness isn't always easy. We may live too fast a lifestyle, even when we retire or are on vacation.

Prayer is what connects our beliefs with our lives.

For example, a bulletin board at a retirement home has thirty-six events scheduled for the coming week; the cruise director announces that for today we have sunrise worship, early morning stretch workout, followed by board games on the deck, followed by mid-morning snacks, followed by group discussion on current events, followed by . . . (Help! Stop the boat! We want to get off!)

A recently published book describes the typical person today as being saturated—filled with information, ideas, plans, worries, and so forth. We are over-scheduled and over-committed. And what will our life be like with the introduction of the additional 500-channel television stations soon to be sending programs into in our homes?

Many of us yearn for moments of quiet reflection. We long for peaceful times when we can pull together the varied strands of our lives. We may not use the word, but what we seek is prayer. Time to reflect; time to quietly talk with our God. We want to connect what was with what is. We want to become more present to ourselves. We want to relax a bit with Someone who loves us and does not judge us. Prayer connects the flow of our

We want to relax . . . with someone who loves us.

life with ourselves; prayer connects the flow of our life with our God; prayer helps us become aware that our God is always present to us.

Some of us get in touch with our lives by talking over our experiences and problems with others. We think out loud because we do better with an audience. The give and take of conversation clarifies things for us. By laying out all the aspects of the problem, we knit together the various aspects of a problem into a pattern that makes sense. We are able to observe ourselves as if from the outside; we gain a new perspective. Sometimes this process of talking and listening is at the heart of professional counseling during which we try to achieve a better understanding of what's happening in our lives.

But our God is always listening. Always there. The One with whom we can always share our problems and thoughts and concerns. God is always a receptive audience; God listens to everything; God is never bored with anything we might say. With God we can "get things off our chest"! We can trust the things that bother us to the bottomless depths of God's love.

God can handle all our anger and grief and pain and loneliness and disappointment. Jesus has told us that the burden will be light if we share it with God. And God longs for our company.

We must not forget, however, that our God is a God of joyfulness! God delights in our happiness. So celebrating our successes with God is natural too! We all like to hear about our loved ones' joys, and God is no exception. God eagerly waits for us to share our happiness!

Meditation and contemplation

Many of us were raised on a tradition of learning and reciting prayers. We memorized the Hail Mary, *God longs for our company.*

grace before meals, and the Act of Contrition. Such traditional prayers serve the wonderful need we have to pray in unison with others. They also serve us well when we can't think of anything to say to God. In times of crisis, memorized prayers come immediately to our mind and provide us with words and thoughts that come from the rich tradition of our faith.

Along with the practice of "saying prayers," our Church also has the rich tradition of mental prayer or meditation. Sometimes we call meditation by another name—contemplation, which involves a deep awareness of God's presence. For instance, we can meditate on the beauty of a clear flowing stream or a gentle snowfall and immediately think of the beauty of God who made the world so wondrous. Or we can simply reflect on the wonder of the universe itself—its incredible size and age, its history and energy. The mystery of the universe and its creator can fill us with awe. This can lead us to become deeply aware not only of creation but also of the creator.

Some writers on prayer call meditation "wordless prayer." It can be relaxing, even playful; it activates our imagination. For example, in our opening story, the Native Americans visiting the burial grounds were connecting themselves with their ancestors, the earth, and the creator of all life. Their rituals awakened these wonderful connections in their imagination. They became quiet; they gathered their thoughts and memories into their hearts; they became more aware of past and present. In other words, they meditated.

We can connect this kind of prayer with family life. Many of us contemplate the mystery of new life or the mystery of love with its inexplicable attraction between people. We wonder at the sharing of ideas, hopes, dreams, pleasure, and even pain, which comes through the encounter of spouses or friends. Mystery surrounds us. All this brings forth a holy act of contemplation.

Even children can experience the joy of meditation and contemplation. In fact, many writers say that children are natural contemplatives who live always with a sense of wonder—until it is trained out of them. A child can spend what seems hours just looking at the clouds or watching a colony of ants go about its daily work. They can stare at the mole on the nose of Aunt Gertrude with fascination and delight. Unless they see too much television or are taught to think linearly and logically, children can retain an imagination that is alive and active. Mystery is woven into the fabric of their lives. (We adults may have to relearn this!)

Thus, children are excellent *pray-ers*. Alert to the wonders of creation, they may respond spontaneously to life's mysteries. A deep awareness of God.

We will explore the prayer life and the spirituality of the family in many different ways in this small book. Here, however, we reflect on the simple fact that in family life we can appreciate one another as incredibly wondrous mysteries who live quite ordinary lives. Like the image of the life-giving blood flowing through our whole system, prayer is the life-blood of our life with God and with our family.

Laughing together over the little things.

Sometimes we shy away from prayer because we were "over-prayed" as kids or we never caught on to the reason for or the how-to of prayer. Whatever the reason, what is important is that prayer is just like a good heart-to-heart talk with an intimate friend, one to whom we can tell anything and everything. Or it's like simply being with one another and saying little or nothing.

Perhaps this person is our husband or our wife, perhaps a sister or parent. Or perhaps, a friend. Learning what prayer is then can come from this similar experience: Sharing time, thoughts, and feelings with a very special person who happens to be on the earth at the same time we are!

Picture this person in your mind. Remember for a moment some of your best times together when you felt the closest. Maybe when you were both relaxing or you were taking a long fun walk; or when you were on the phone for hours. Remember those times when you felt that no one else existed in the world; those times when you knew that you needed no one else; those times when the two of you were one. (*Pause and remember.*)

That's like prayer. Just you and God in deep relationship, in deep conversation. Laughing together over the little things, discussing the fact that taxes are due and you don't know when you'll do them. Deciding what to have for supper or how to talk about something important with a spouse or whether to plant petunias or daisies. Big and little stuff. The stuff of close intimate friends. God stuff. Holy stuff.

However, we don't need to dial God at the office or look for God in another room or drive over to God's house. God is right here, within us, around us, by us, for us. God is totally available to us in each and every moment of each and every day. And God listens with full attention as if we were the only person in the whole, wide world. And we are present to God! God's nature is to be totally present to each of us all the time. No matter what. God is here. God is now.

Maybe you pray often; maybe you pray only once in a while in church or in the bathroom or wherever. (Actually, studies show that the two most popular places to pray are in the car and in the bathroom.) But wherever or whenever you pray, consider increasing the times you're present to your God. Add one more time a week or a day or an hour. Maybe God has been trying to talk with you all through the reading of this chapter. Perhaps you could let go of all the noise in your head. And just listen.

A Psalm

I will remember your great deeds, Lord;
I will recall the wonders you did in the past.
I will think about all that you have done;
I will meditate on all your mighty acts.

Psalm 77:11–12

Family Quietivity

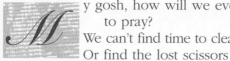y gosh, how will we ever find time
          to pray?
          We can't find time to clean the garage
          Or find the lost scissors
Or write thank-you notes
Or make important arrangements
Like doctor appointments!
Finding any extra time is next to impossible!
Groceries have to be bought every week!
And each of us is going in a hundred
    different directions.

Pray?
We do—every week, in church.
And when we finally sit down
    for a good family dinner,
We pray.
It's too hard to think about finding more time.
There's too much else going on.
Barely time for any peace and quiet.
God will understand.
God knows how busy we are.
God knows.

Excuse me?
Prayer can be a part of all we do?
A natural part?
Well, God knows that's simple enough!

CHAPTER TWO
Prayer Connects with Ordinary Life

We bless the beginning of the day with our good morning.

Not having been able to get back to sleep, he decided to get up. At least he could make the coffee. The birds were chirping, so he knew the sun would be up any minute. Once the coffee-maker was set, he opened the patio door to get some fresh air and then, on second thought, decided to go out into the quiet, damp experience of dawn.

He was taken with the sweet smell of night leaving and the day awaking. The thought came to mind that this was almost as if someone were lifting a soft blanket that covered the scent of day from their small back yard.

"How great it is out here" he thought. "Especially now, with the world asleep. It's amazing that this experience is here, every day, every morning, and none of us gets up to enjoy it."

Going in to get a cup of coffee, he knew everyone else would stay in bed on this Saturday morning. No reason to get up. It was the only day they could just be family and enjoy some leisure time to do that. Every other day was planned for them by some other institution—work, school, parish.

Taking his coffee back to his holy place, he sat down on a slightly damp plastic lawn chair. He didn't care about getting his jeans wet. Here he had time to think, time just to be himself. "Oh, Lord," he said out loud, "how great this is to just sit in the quiet."

Then he heard the birds. They had been chirping all along, but suddenly he heard each individual sound. And he chuckled to himself, thinking God was talking to him.

"Good morning to you too," he said out loud.

He must have been out there a full hour, because pretty soon he began to hear noises in the kitchen and their youngest poked her head around and said "Mornin', Daddy."

"Mornin', Trisha."

"Mommy up yet?" she asked.

"Don't think so; get some cereal and c'mon out," he answered.

Then he heard her say "Good morning" again.

And his wife answered her, "Good morning."

Suddenly his reflective mood grabbed onto those words. "They're just like the birds! Birds chirp the morning into sunrise; we do the same thing! We bless the beginning of the day with our good morning to each other," he thought. What wonderful words! A statement—Have a good morning! A wonderful statement about the reality of right now and about the hope and expectation of the day! Almost a prayer!

"Of course," he suddenly realized, "it is a prayer! A connecting with one another, with the day, with our hope for this day and for tomorrow. A prayer of hope and openness!"

"Boy, I never thought about that before," he heard himself say out loud.

"You say something?" his wife said as she stuck her head around the corner of the patio door.

"I said good morning," he answered.

After the Sabbath was over, Mary Magdalene, Mary
the mother of James, and Salome bought spices
to go and anoint the body of Jesus. Very early on
Sunday morning, at sunrise, they went to the tomb.
On the way they said to one another, "Who will
roll away the stone for us from the entrance to
the tomb?" (It was a very large stone.) Then they
looked up and saw that the stone had already been
rolled back. So they entered the tomb, where they
saw a young man sitting at the right, wearing a
white robe—and they were alarmed.

Don't be alarmed," he said. "I know you are
looking for Jesus of Nazareth, who was crucified.
He is not here—he has been raised! Look, here
is the place where he was placed. Now go and give
this message to his disciples, including Peter: 'He is
going to Galilee ahead of you; there you will see
him, just as he told you.' "

Mark 16:1–7

_____ **🔖**

*God listens to the
murmurs of our heart.*

🔖
_____

Morning has dawned;
time to pay attention to
the new day. The day is
coming; it's beginning.
Let's awaken from our
sleep; let's awaken to the
reality of our lives! Let's enter the day with anticipation,
with eagerness, and with as little anxiety as possible!
Rejoice! Alleluia! A new day has dawned!

Let's step into the new day of the gospel story. Jesus'
women friends probably did not wake up this morning
with many good feelings. They had a hard night.
Coming to the tomb at morning had probably been hard
for them because their leader and friend was brutally
murdered on Friday. He was gone from them.

They probably hadn't slept since then. But part of the reality of their life and their custom was the anointing of the body on the third day. So they woke to their task, to the leftover stuff that helps life go on. Their hearts were heavy, much as we in a family feel when we have to make arrangements at a funeral parlor. Doing so is part of our ordinary life, but we dread its reality.

We all know what facing another day is like. The events of the past determine the expectation or dread of our awakening. The husband and father in our opening story must have had a good day the day before. His awakening is gentle, and he's able to enter the day in a slow and easy way.

We all like days like that. Days when we're able to reflect on the birds and say good morning. Days when we recognize these actions as our prayers. Days when we recognize the holiness of connecting with God through the ordinary events of our life.

God waits for us to share our day—at the beginning, in the middle, at the end—whenever we suddenly feel the urge to say hello. In the ordinary messiness of our real lives, we seek our God, and God waits for us—eager, expectant, smiling.

God listens to the murmurs of our heart; God stays tuned in to us. In prayer, we tune in to God. We tell our story and then we listen to the love that pours forth from God, who treasures us.

In prayer we need to listen. Why? Because without listening, how can we ever hear the tears and laughter and concern and love of our God?

_____ ✌️ _____

Listening requires more energy than speaking.

_____ ✌️ _____

We each have two ears and one mouth. This is God's way of reminding us that we should listen twice as much as we speak! Well, not exactly, but no real conversation ever happens without good listening. And to listen well is no easy task.

First, we have to want to listen. We need to value the word, the idea, or the opinion of another person. Listening is not simply waiting to get the next word in; it's not musing over what we will say when this person speaking to us finally finishes; it's not conjuring up the definitive word or the best argument or the clincher.

No. Listening is an action, just as speaking is. Some of us who are parents have learned the skill of active listening. Totally tuned into the full message of the child, we strain to hear the barely audible fear or hurt that is embedded in the words of the child or teen. Listening requires an active posture; it requires an attention that often takes more energy than speaking.

When we listen, we seek to orient or focus our awareness on what's outside ourselves. We quiet the interior noise and position our receptors to what's being broadcast out there. Our focus moves from self to others, from ourselves to the one doing the talking.

In prayer, we need to listen well—to God, to others, to ourselves. Good listening grounds us in reality. Prayerful listening connects us with the real God and not with some creation of our imagination.

God's revelation and prayer
When we talk about God communicating with us, we're also talking about God's word. John's Gospel begins with the dramatic statement that Jesus is the Word of God.

This Word—the person of Jesus—contains the truth of God. Jesus embodies the content of God's revelation. If we ask God, "What are you like?" God would probably say, "Here, I'll show you." and then point to Jesus.

So we learn about God by hearing the Word of God, that is, by listening to and learning from Jesus. And just as the active listening mentioned above takes great energy, so does listening to Jesus. To hear the Word of God means we possess an open mind.

Hear the footsteps of the creator.

We allow Jesus to break through any preconceptions we have about God.

Jesus faced this problem in his earthly ministry. Many came to him seeking something or someone else. They sought what some call a political messiah who would destroy the enemies of Israel and bring them the political freedom and dominance they had experienced during the time of King David. But Jesus has come as one who is more interested in serving than in being served. He comes as one who loves, instead of destroying so-called enemies.

During his time on earth, many of his listeners did not want to hear Jesus' words of love and peace, and they left him. Even those closest to him did not appear at first to accept his suffering and crucifixion. They liked to hear about the abundant life of the kingdom, but not about the seeming negatives connected with it. They found many of his sayings "hard" for he asked them to be generous to all and to love everyone—friend and foe alike.

This is the Word of God; this is the Word we listen to when we pray.

Prayer as careful listening

God is present everywhere. If we listen to nature with very attentive ears, we may hear the footsteps of the creator. God is also present in people. If we listen to the deeper cares and concerns of others, we hear the echo of God's invitation to love. God is present in Sacred Scripture and if we listen carefully not only to what is in the lines but also to what happens between the lines, we will clearly hear the voice of our God.

As Catholics, we also have the rich treasures of our tradition—our teachings, sacraments, prayers, and so forth. Again, the Word of God is within these traditions. However, we have to get beyond the surface of things to draw forth the spiritual richness within. Again, we need attentive listening without prejudgment.

A special setting for prayer is the celebration of the liturgy. In the eucharistic liturgy both the word of God and the body of Christ nourish us. A passive attitude during Mass will not break open the reality of God's love. Straining to listen, quieting the noise within us, hearing, reflecting, and thinking are all part of receiving God's word addressed directly to us.

From the posture of listening arises the invitation for response. We remember, too, that when the formal church liturgy proclaims the word of God, we listen not just to the word of the lector (reader) or priest, but to God who communicates through them. Even the rustle of the bulletin, the crying of children, the whispered conversation three pews ahead can be, if we are open to them, communications from our God.

A wonderful traditional practice of our Church is called *lectio divina*, or the reading of divine things. Usually this involves the quiet and prayerful reading of Scripture. The pace is slow; the mood, pensive. The goal is not to read quickly and finish the passage.

Rather it is to open ourselves to the words of Scripture, allowing them to penetrate our imagination, our emotions, and our mind.

A few words read in this spirit are worth more than hundreds or thousands of words read quickly. We are not involved in speed-reading. Hearing, accepting, and living one genuine word of God is better than listening to millions of words read with divided attention.

To really learn about the deep truth in ourselves or other people, we listen very carefully. We learn to listen with our heart. And when we listen with our heart, we hear the deepest reality. When we pray, we actively listen both to God and to ourselves. Then, if we listen well, we will hear both the voice of God and the hunger of our own heart.

"Prayer in the events of each day and each moment is one of the secrets of the kingdom revealed. . . ."

CCC, 2660

---
*God waits at every big
and little crossroad.*

In one of his poems, Robert Frost uses two images: that of two roads diverging in the woods and that of the choice we have to make to take one or the other. The road we choose, especially if it is the one less traveled, makes all the difference.

We are blessed to have our God's help when we reach one of those crossroads, one of those choices. Decisions aren't easy, and depending on the complexity or the importance of a decision, they are sometimes heart wrenching. We are torn between two or more options. And since we cannot know the future, we can't see beyond the bend in each road.

Carefully weighing the possible outcomes and deciding in our mind and heart to move toward one takes a lot of trust. We trust in our own abilities to think through something and to carry out our decision. We trust that we can live with and accept the consequences of our decision.

Trust involves faith, and that's where our God comes in again. God waits, quietly and patiently, at every big and little crossroad or decision in our lives. God waits, always eager and anxious to listen to us as we talk through our decision. God listens and then speaks; we speak and then listen! And God delights as we listen with an open heart to the possibilities that prayer offers us.

What a wonderful thought! We have someone who will listen and help us through our difficulties. And, unlike us, God does know what's beyond each bend in the road! What wonderful advice God can give!

Sometimes God speaks to us through others. This way, God helps us make big decisions and small, ordinary ones.

In our opening story, the exchange of good mornings was a message from God—a reminder, a wake-up call from God. "Yes, this is a good morning!" Implied within this greeting is the thought, "Let's make it a good day!"

The next time you wish others a "good morning," remember that this is a prayer for them and for yourself. Be aware that God is listening and wants us to have a good day! God is eager for the day to go well. God longs for our day to be filled with goodness and blessings. And perhaps, when someone wishes you a good morning, you might listen well and be daring and answer, "Amen." (So be it!)

> *"The* Christian family *is the first place of education in prayer. Based on the sacrament of marriage, the family is the 'domestic church' where God's children learn to pray 'as the Church' and to persevere in prayer. For young children . . . , daily family prayer is the first witness of the Church's living memory . . ."*
>
> CCC, 2685

A Psalm

I am listening to what the Lord God is saying;
    he promises peace to us, his own people.
    if we do not go back to our foolish ways.
Surely he is ready to save those who honor him.
    and his saving presence will remain in our land.
Love and faithfulness will meet righteousness and peace
    will embrace.
Human loyalty will reach up from the earth,
    and God's righteousness will look down from heaven.

From Psalm 85:8–11

Heart Talk

'*ve* never done this before, God,
Just sat, waiting for you.
I always thought that prayer
    was me talking—
Not both of us.
So this is new, but they tell me you understand.
They tell me you know everything about me.
I guess I knew that in my heart.

In my heart—
Yes, that's where I know these things
Even if they're hard to believe sometimes
And I have to listen closely
Or do a lot of thinking
(A lot of thinking!)
About some of them,
But in my heart I *know.*

Is that where you are, God?
Are you there?

Oh, I forgot!
I have to keep quiet and listen
So you can speak.
I'm sorry.
Forgive me.
Now, go ahead . . .
Amen.

CHAPTER THREE
The Prayer of Acceptance and Our Spirituality

Thea had an uncanny ability to find that one person who most needed her attention.

She walked to the podium, and once the applause had subsided, she began.

"I want to talk to you about a very holy person I know," she told the group of adults gathered to hear her speak. "Her name is Thea Bowman. *Sister* Thea Bowman. And she is no longer alive, but I still know her. And I want to talk a little bit about that as we begin our experience tonight,

"Sister Thea Bowman died of a very painful cancer a few years ago. At the prime of her life, we might say. One of the most gifted persons and presenters I have ever experienced. Why? Because she was just herself. She sang some of the old spirituals, she talked in between, and she used the wonderful dialect of her southern and African roots to capture and enthrall those who came to be with her. And her words were profound. They resound in my ears still.

"Thea had an uncanny ability to find that one person or two or ten in the room who most needed her attention. And she did this with her eyes. Connecting and reconnecting. Until her presence overcame them. The presence of God in Thea Bowman.

"She did this to me, and then zapped me with words that went something like this: 'After my family would come back from church on Sunday. Y'know what I mean? All dressed up, n' all, and be glad we were home agin'? Then what would happen was, we'd come home and *do church!* We'd come home and jest do it. We'd *be* church. N' somehow, I think that the most important things that happened, that God paid the most attention to, was when we *did* church there at home.'

"Thea Bowman changed my life that day. I went to my old family home, even though my parents had died long ago, shortly after I entered the convent. And I just sat there in front of the old family house.

"And I remembered *doing* church with my family. I realized how much I didn't do that anymore. How I barely saw them. How I missed them. Then I sat there, and I talked to my deceased mom and dad. And all the while, I recognized these moments as holy. Holy. A prayer between my family and me. God was very much in the midst of us.

"And my prayer life is now all a part of my everyday experiences. There is hardly a separation between what I do and the fact that my God is a part of it. I am aware of the holiness of what happens.

"Now I'm not saying that I think about God all the time. No way. But I know God is always thinking about me. I am never alone, even when I prefer to be. God is with me, in how I work and how I pray, in how I enjoy life, in how I get impatient and crabby, and even in how I play. Because I simply remember Thea is about God's presence in the ordinary things we do.

She ended this opening to her short presentation, took a breath and suddenly realized that no one had moved.

"Lord," she said out loud, "we feel your presence here in our midst. Be with us as we speak and as we listen. Help us to recognize you in our midst, both here and when we leave. Help us be church. Thank you, Lord." And she felt the presence of God and of Thea.

Jesus went into Jericho and was passing through. There was a chief tax collector there named Zacchaeus, who was rich. He was trying to see who Jesus was, but he was a little man and could not see Jesus because of the crowd. So he ran ahead of the crowd and climbed a sycamore tree to see Jesus, who was going to pass that way. When Jesus came to that place, he looked up and said to Zacchaeus. "Hurry down, Zacchaeus, because I must stay in your house today."

Zacchaeus hurried down and welcomed him with great joy. All the people who saw it started grumbling. "This man has gone as a guest to the home a sinner!"

Zacchaeus stood up and said to the Lord, "Listen, sir! I will give half my belongings to the poor, and if I have cheated anyone, I will pay back four times as much."

Jesus said to him, "Salvation has come to this house today, for this man, also, is a descendant of Abraham. The Son of Man came to seek and to save the lost."

Luke 19:1–10

_____ Sometimes God spots us
up in a tree, as Jesus
God continues to laugh spotted Zacchaeus. No
and cry and enjoy with us. matter where we are
_____ perched or how far out on
the limb we are, God's
understanding eyes are on us. Zacchaeus, a tax collector (one of the most despised jobs in Jesus' days), thought he was just going to watch this man called Jesus pass by. But no. Jesus paid attention to him, called him down from his limb, and then invited himself to Zacchaeus's home.

Thus, does Jesus teach us. God knows exactly where we are in our lives. God even knows when we decide to turn away from our true selves. Yet, God continues to stay with us, to break bread at our tables, to sleep in our beds, to laugh and cry and enjoy with us. All we need do is accept God's presence. And we do this through prayer—all sorts of prayer at all sorts of times.

Zacchaeus accepted Jesus' invitation to be with him. And Zacchaeus's acceptance of Jesus' invitation changed the tax collector's life and the lives of others. His decision to be open to an active relationship with Jesus forever changed the story of his life.

Zacchaeus probably had what we'd call a "big" conversion experience. We wonder why he didn't fall out of the tree and onto the ground! Some of us do. The woman in our opening story had a similar experience. God singled her out through Thea Bowman. The woman accepted it and was forever changed.

When something like this happens within our lives and our hearts, we want to give thanks. God has answered our prayers; our lives have changed. Everything is much, much better. Gratitude swells our hearts. The world seems better, no matter what is happening. And we offer a prayer of thanks to our God who makes all things possible.

The woman in our opening story does this over and over as she shares the stories of her faith conversions. A simple, honest, accepting prayer. All we have to do is accept God's acceptance of us. All we need do is believe in God's love, God's compassionate love for us.

Sounds easy, doesn't it? Not really. The most difficult kind of acceptance is self-acceptance. God invites us to accept our history, our talents and lack thereof, our looks, our personality, our flaws, our faults, our virtues, our strengths, and on and on. The whole of us.

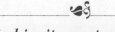

God invites us to accept the whole of us.

We all know that life is never perfect. Nor are we. But we also live with a hope that things can be different. And some things can change, but much of who we are and many of the circumstances of our lives are simply givens. They will never change. They are part of the gift of life that God has given us. So sometimes we feel restless and angry about the hand we think God has dealt us. Our prayer of acceptance rises from this tension between what is and what isn't within us.

One of the most quoted prayers ever composed was written by Reinhold Niebuhr, a great Protestant theologian of the twentieth century. Many of us know the first lines of this prayer, which was eventually named "The Serenity Prayer," because it is one of those prayers that we often see in gift shops. The Serenity Prayer begins,

> God, grant me the serenity to accept the things that I cannot change; courage to change the things I can; and wisdom to know the difference.

The wonderful part of this prayer is that it applies to almost everything in our life. *Almost* everything— because some things in our life should be changed! For example, our human dignity deserves, even demands, the respect of others. Therefore, when someone puts us down, mistreats us, abuses us in any way, we never have to simply accept this as part of our life. Never.

Let's notice that the Serenity Prayer says "to change the things I can." Part of our responsibility is to change, to work against, the evil that is within our power to change. We must do whatever we can. Our God calls us to that.

When we can change evil into good (for example, doing all we can to reconcile a child with a parent who has abandoned the family), we are making the world a better

It is the story of Jesus.
It is our story.

place. For everyone. However, we sometimes find that having "the wisdom to know the difference" in what we can or cannot change is very difficult. This wisdom, together with the energy and the plain old guts to make the change, can come from prayer. All of this—*all of this*—is part of the struggle of being Christian. It is the story of Jesus. It is our story.

God is actively involved in our lives. God's word, as it comes to us in the Scriptures and through our Church, challenges us to accept the things we cannot change and to change the things we can. The story of Zacchaeus in the New Testament shows us someone accepting this challenge.

During his career as a tax collector, Zacchaeus may have used the clout associated with his profession for his own advantage. In those days, the Romans assigned a certain quota of taxes for each tax collector to raise; everything they collected above that amount, the tax collectors kept. If people didn't pay, the tax collector had to answer to the local Roman forces. The system begged to be abused! Note that the writer of Luke's gospel tells us that Zacchaeus was very rich!

Because Zacchaeus was a tax collector, he probably thought of himself as a sinner. (Others certainly thought of him that way!) But Jesus did not see Zacchaeus that way. He saw the deep down goodness in this man sitting up on that limb and invited himself to dinner at Zacchaeus's home. As a new friend of Jesus, Zacchaeus would choose to change; he'd choose to accept a new way of being. And his path to change was made easier because he knew that Jesus believed in him.

The Good News is that God accepts us; the "bad news" (not really) is that we must accept ourselves. And who are we? People God loves throughout eternity. Forever. No matter what. People God accepts in each and every moment of each and every day.

Mary's deep prayer of acceptance

Most of us have heard the story of the angel's visit to Mary to announce the coming of Jesus. When God sends messengers, they usually seem to bring challenges of rather large proportion. Thus, Luke, the Gospel writer, notes that Mary is both confused and afraid. Probably more of the latter.

The angel seeks to console her. No pressure, but God does have a request of Mary. We know what it is. God invites Mary to be the mother of the messiah (which means "the one sent"). Perhaps she might harbor some serious reservations. She might inquire whether she has a second choice. Maybe she might say that she has to sleep on the question and will get back to the angel with an answer tomorrow.

We don't know all the details. All we are given in the Gospel account is her Yes: "I am the Lord's servant. May it happen to me as you have said." (Luke 1:38) In the Latin version of the biblical text "may it happen" or "let it happen" is the word *fiat*. Thus Mary's response is sometimes simply called Mary's fiat. Our tradition offers this fiat to us as both an example and a model of a prayer that accepts God's will.

When we pray this prayer, we are like Mary. We accept whatever God wants of us. We do this with openness and freedom; we allow ourselves to be vulnerable to God's wishes. In a sense, we give back to God the life God has given us. This act of acceptance is no small matter. Of all the prayers we might express, it is among the most significant.

Once Mary's initial acceptance is given, the matter is not finished. She has agreed to be the mother of Jesus. But does she know all that will happen down the road? Probably not. She probably learns life as it unfolds about and around and within her. God invites her many more times to renew her original fiat. She says yes to her son being a wandering preacher; yes to his remaining unmarried and to having no children or grandchildren for her.

Mary says yes to Jesus' growing popularity that took him away from her; yes to the mounting religious and political opposition poised against him; yes to the possibility of his impending death; yes to his suffering; yes to the actuality of his death. Mary said yes to her life.

The accepting prayer of Jesus

Maybe she has to sleep on the question.

Mary's prayer of acceptance comes from early in her life; the most meaningful of acceptance prayers from Jesus happened toward the end of his life.

The setting is dramatic; the personal anguish of Jesus apparent. Kneeling in the garden of the Mount of Olives, he prays, "Father, if you will, take this cup of suffering away from me. Not my will, however, but your will be done." (Luke 22:42)

Jesus begins his prayer with the address he taught others to use in prayer. Jesus encourages us to call God forth into our presence by using God's name: *Abba*, Daddy. With these symbolic words, Jesus points out God's closeness and care. In the best of all possible worlds, these are words of intimacy and trust.

Trust is the deeper meaning of the prayer of acceptance. The future appears dark and dangerous, perhaps even destructive of things good and beautiful. People could get hurt; we could be hurt. Is it wise for us to take this route? The situation invites trust, especially when we know little about what is ahead.

We'd be foolish if we were accepting of something from the hand of someone hostile or indifferent toward us. But that is not the way of our God. Jesus could say his prayer of acceptance, difficult as it was, because he knew God as *Abba*. God would not destroy him but would always be a God of life.

When we accept, we give God permission to unfold the rest of the drama that is our life. We continue to participate in this mystery of life. We embrace it, cherish it, and give our energy to it—even though our life may at times seem to be something we cannot entirely understand. We accept life's events as they come to us, flowing from the will of a loving God. A very loving God.

Acceptance, gladness, and thanksgiving

A sure sign of whether our acceptance is real is the attitude we have toward life. If we are sad and depressed, if we complain all the time, most likely we have not said a prayer of acceptance with our whole being. We have not meant what we prayed. Maybe we said the words, but our heart was not in the words. Of course, sometimes all we can do at a time in our lives when all seems dark is to make a decision to accept, grit our teeth, and then move ahead. And God understands.

A sure sign of full acceptance is that our heart says yes and our emotions follow. And what finally comes forth is a genuine sense of thanksgiving. Hard as saying yes is, or easy as it is, we say our fiat and we are grateful for what comes to be. We are challenged to be more fully human, more fully alive.

This does not mean that life is good only when it is difficult. Jesus enjoyed a good meal or even a party! He probably had a good time at the home of Zacchaeus!

Maybe a better time than his host. But, as we know, the will of God tends to be balanced in that we are offered times of both pain and times of pleasure. And God desires our wholehearted acceptance of both.

The story of Sister Thea Bowman is a wonderful story of acceptance. Her life by today's standards was cut short. Cancer came to take her from us right at the time when we seemed to most need her vision and her voice. Unlike anyone else, she could express the beauty of Catholicism as it is lived in the African-American culture. She was a prophetess, a witness to life.

As the cancer moved to take life from her body, Sister Thea kept her smile and her ministry a hummin.' Thousands of Catholics and non-Catholics traveled great distances to hear her message, especially as she expressed it through her powerful spirituals. Toward the end, she could no longer walk and someone had to wheel her onto the stage or into the sanctuary. Having lost her hair through chemotherapy, she wrapped her head in wonderful colored cloth reminiscent of her African heritage!

Suffering and joy need not be opposites.

All who met her knew that she was at peace with her God. A sense of joy and thanksgiving emanated from her. Yes, she had accepted the mystery of life and the mystery of death. And both mysteries dwelt with her. She showed how suffering and joy were not opposites.

In her life and death, she touched others—including us—as we struggle to accept our own lives.

God will not give us something that is not do-able.

Getting up on a Saturday morning and accepting that we're out of milk or eggs or cereal is easy if we know we can fix the situation. But accepting something that we can't fix is not so easy. Perhaps we can't put food on the table because we don't have any money. Or maybe even a kitchen.

Being able to accept our lives is all relative to what we must accept. For example, accepting the death of a child is one of the most difficult realities we can imagine. But people do it. With terrible agony and pain, yes, but they somehow manage to say yes. Still, they reserve the right to ask "Why?" when they finally see God face to face.

Accepting other losses such as our home to fire or flood also is hard. But relative to the fact that our family may have survived, accepting the loss of replaceable things becomes easier, or at least, do-able.

We don't understand a lot about life. Divorce and the pain it brings a family is hard for us to understand for it is a death of a different sort. And the history of the not-yet-born nor conceived members of that family are affected forever. Yet many people accept the pain, live through it, and come out on the other side stronger and more accepting of life. They're still family; they still have loving relationships; they are still church. Life goes on—is do-able.

God wants us to know that God will not give us something that is not do-able. We can become better persons through some terrible reality in our lives. We do this all the time. And through these challenges, God invites us to come closer. We accept that God knows the answer to our question "why?"

As you've read this chapter, you have perhaps been feeling the pain or anguish of something you have experienced on your life's journey. Something that you have had to accept; that you cannot change. Perhaps a death. Perhaps a job loss. Perhaps hopes or dreams of a certain nature.

Our God waits to talk with you about this. God has ways to help you work through your pain, accept the whole thing, and even perhaps some day feel good about what is now happening. You can believe this. In so doing, you have already said the first word of the prayer of acceptance—Amen. So it is. So may it be.

"Jesus also prays for us—in our place and on our behalf. All our petitions were gathered up, once for all, in his cry on the Cross and, in his Resurrection, heard by the Father."

CCC, 2741

A Psalm

How good it is to give thanks to you, O Lord,
  to sing in your honor, O Most High God,
to proclaim your constant love every morning
  and your faithfulness every night,
with the music of stringed instruments
  and with melody on the harp.
Your mighty deeds, O Lord, make me glad;
  because of what you have done, I sing for joy.

Psalm 92:1–4

Not So Easy

We have to be honest, God,
      Because that's the way you want us to be.
      Giving thanks for something that is
            hard to accept is not easy!
Plain and simple, God,
The last thing we want to do is to suggest
That we would welcome more pain or problems.
We are only human, you know.

It doesn't encourage us much
When we do have strong faith in the power of prayer
And how much you care,
And you answer "No."
It's just so hard,
Not to get what we want.
What we want.
What we want.
And to accept the answer.

We don't understand everything about being God.
But we're trying,
And we'll keep on trying.
And we know that since you can see around the bend
    in the road,
You know what's ahead.
And we don't.

Amen.

CHAPTER FOUR

Yearning to Know Our God Better

"Ain't that somethin'?"

The beach was packed with people. They didn't usually head out for a walk when the crowd was so large, but today they needed to do that. When they reached the water's edge, which seemed to take them longer each time, they turned, as always, to walk along the shore. Walking in the wet sand was easier because it was smooth and firm. If one wanted to walk the beach and not work so hard, one walked on the wet sand.

Their steps were slower this summer. She noticed it especially of him, and supposed they were just going to keep getting slower. They weren't exactly spring chickens anymore!

She watched the sand directly in front of them as they walked. People always do this, she suddenly realized, watch the sand they are stepping onto. At least, she always did. Once in a while she glanced up at a family picnicking on a blanket or at the sun bathers or out into the water to watch those finding delight by jumping in the waves.

And once in a while, she even glanced up toward the sky or out into the ocean itself. But this was only if something caught her eye, like a passing plane following the shore or a kite or even seagulls. Rarely did she look out to the horizon, to the fine line dividing water from sky.

If she did, it wasn't for long. For the horizon didn't hold her attention.

"Look at that little one there," her husband suddenly said, pointing to a two- or three-year-old little girl, dressed in a bright bathing suit and holding a shovel and pail. Crouched down with her little behind just touching the water, she was piling wet sand, over-flowing the bucket.

"She'll go far in life," he continued. "She won't be held back. No limits. Get all the sand in you can, then some more! Too many people in life don't try. She's doin' it. Ain't that somethin' "?

His wisdom touched her heart, and she found his arm and moved closer. Then, though her eyes now blurred from her own tears, she purposefully looked out to the horizon. "There," she thought, "there at that fine line where the heavens meet the earth, is the line we will someday cross. One of us first, and then the other. And there, just on the other side, we'll meet.

"I hope he goes first," she thought. "He's more ready than I."

> *"The* Christian family *is the first place of education in prayer."*
>
> CCC, 2685

Once a man came to Jesus, "Teacher," he asked, "what good thing must I do to receive eternal life?"

"Why do you ask me concerning what is good?" answered Jesus. "There is only One who is good. Keep the commandments if you want to enter life."

"I have obeyed all these commandments," the young man replied. "What else do I need to do?"

Jesus said to him, "If you want to be perfect, go and sell all you have and give the money to the poor, and you will have riches in heaven; then come and follow me."

When the young man heard this, he went away sad, because he was very rich.   *Matthew 19:16–17, 20–22*

We could leave it all behind.

Yike! Do you suppose Jesus meant exactly what he said in this gospel passage? If so, some of us are in deep trouble! Especially since he implies that owning anything threatens our eternal life. But Jesus is obviously giving us a deeper meaning here. The young man is yearning for more, wanting something else. (That old hunger we've talked about so often in this familystyle catechism.)

So what is Jesus saying here? Maybe that the young man's craving to acquire more stuff and even more recognition for his having kept all the commandments is off base. Real fulfillment may involve being so unattached to things of this world that we could give up everything. Everything! We could leave it all behind.

We'd leave behind all those cars, stereos, houses, clothes, bank accounts—everything we've collected to satisfy our yearning. And then, after we've done that (perhaps even gone so far as to have a garage sale to get rid of some of these things and then given the money from the sale to the poor!), then, and only then, will we be open enough to have all our dreams come true.

People who have had a near-death experience say that they move toward light. And when they return to us, they are changed. They no longer live their lives exactly the same. They lose their strong attachment to things of this world. And what becomes important to them? Building relationships; spending time with loved ones; working with the sick, the dying, the poor; making a difference in the world. All these interests become important, and central to their lives.

Another universal change that result from these near-death experiences is that those who have them lose their fear of death. They know they are not finished living their life here on earth; they accept the reality that when they complete their lives here, they will get to go on—to the light.

The elderly couple in our opening story seem to have become unattached to worldly things. They are near the end of their family life; they are ready, even waiting, for the next life. They may fear the life waiting for them; they may wonder sometimes if it even exists. Still, they accept the life they have lived and look forward to something beyond.

Their lives seem fulfilled as they stroll the beach, observing the wonders around them. And still, they yearn for more, knowing that one of them may go on before the other. In wonderful aged-wisdom, the woman believes her husband is more ready than she; she is willing to give him up for the sake of the promise of the next life. In prayer, she recognizes his readiness.

Would that we all reach the point in life reached by this wonderful couple! The point where we love enough to be willing to suffer the pain of a loved one's death, knowing that our God is just on the other side to welcome him or her and, in time (God's time), to welcome us.

_____🔊_____

Jesus was always asking for something.

_____🔊_____

We have all wished upon a star. We've asked for a better place to live, a new love, a better job, better friends, or whatever. We live with a wish in our heart, or we are not completely alive. And God places that wish, that yearning for more, in us as part of our standard equipment.

We came into our life hungry for food and hungry for human contact. Later we add other hungers. Unsatisfied, we walk the path of our life. Our hungers creep into our wish lists and seep into our prayer life. We learn that having needs is all right and that asking for satisfaction of our needs is okay too.

But eventually we come to know, however dimly, that just as we are born with a yearning, so too will we die with a wish within us. We may look back upon our lives with a sense of satisfaction, a sense that we received almost everything we ever wanted, but in full honesty, we will also say, "I still want more."

To attempt to smother our yearning or to ignore our wishes is to violate who God created us to be. God desires to create a need within us, a want, a wish, a hunger within us so that eventually we will move toward that for which we were made in the first place—our God.

Some religions seek to quiet these yearnings in a process aimed at attaining a peacefulness within. But Christianity takes another approach to life, an approach that blesses desire and sanctifies yearning. We reflect on life and when we add up all that this life could ever give, we do not find that all our yearnings have been fulfilled. One of the first words we learn as babies is the word *more*. When we reach the end of our life, in our heart will still be the same sentiment: More!

Yearning for the kingdom

Our hunger creeps into our wish lists.

Nested in the Our Father (the Lord's Prayer), which Jesus taught us, is a set of requests or petitions. Jesus asked for these actions to come about and invites us to ask too. So, we ask God to make the kingdom happen.

Is there some contradiction, some spiritual conflict between what we discussed in the last chapter (the prayer of acceptance) and this prayer of yearning and petition? Shouldn't we just accept what comes to us and be satisfied? Isn't that what we heard as children? "Eat what's on your plate and be grateful."

Remember Jesus' prayer of acceptance on the night before he died. We need to note carefully what Jesus said. He did not start with a prayer of acceptance. He started with a request. He wished that God would remove from his life the horrible death that awaited him on the morrow; he didn't want to die.

We have a name for those who desire pain and suffering simply as pain and suffering. We call them masochists; we also call them mentally ill. We were not created to suffer, but to live.

Jesus was always asking for something. He yearned for friends, for companions along his life's journey. He obviously wanted to eat with others and showed up at more than one banquet. He also prayed that health be restored to many he met. He was a person of needs and desires and dreams. And while the temptation stories in the Gospels may lead us to conclude that Jesus did not want power, prestige, or wealth, they should not make us think that Jesus was without desires. He could not, and neither can we, avoid certain desires.

Of course, not every desire is a good one; that is, not every desire brings about a deepening of God's presence in our lives. Desires for excessive amounts of anything are usually distorted desires. A desire for power can easily mean that we want to use or control others. A desire for prestige can mean that we want to be superior to others. A desire for wealth can mean that we hunger for personal gratification or self-centeredness, without any limits. The desires of Jesus were not like these.

The greatest desire of Jesus was for the kingdom to come. Here! Now! And so he prayed. In the Lord's Prayer we ask God to accomplish all that God desires to accomplish on our behalf. After all, the kingdom is not for God, but for us!

God knows what is best for us because we are foremost in God's thoughts. God is thinking of us, each of us, all the time, each and every moment. Asking God for the kingdom is the same as asking God to provide all of us with that life for which we were made in the first place!

We want the kingdom of God's love here and now; we want it later too. But what we ask for here is not the same as what we hope for later. The couple walking along the beach in our opening story know this. They know that here they have known some goodness and joy; later they will experience unlimited love. This love will invade them (and us), pervade them (and us), fill them (and us)! In the kingdom, they—and we—will know and be known in this love.

The kingdom will not be fully established on this side of life. But it will be when we cross over! To paraphrase Saint Paul in the New Testament: none of our eyes have ever seen such beauty and none of our ears have ever heard such wondrous sounds as God has prepared for us once we die. We live now in hope, but once we live totally and completely with love, we will no longer need. Eternity will be one incredible experience of love.

God enjoys hearing us ask for the kingdom to come here and now. And God will provide all that is needed from God's side to make that happen. God's generosity knows no limits. We may not be able to grasp what kind of measuring cups and spoons God uses, but God's love is always full-measure, even overflowing!

Part of the power of the prayer of yearning or petition is that it places our desires on the tips of our tongues. Then, once expressed, they bounce off the other end of the universe and come back to us—like a boomerang! If we really want something, we have to do our part, God won't do it all. We must get to work ourselves.

If we pray to God to alleviate world hunger and neglect to donate food to the local food shelf, something is wrong! So we must be careful about what we request. A hidden clause, sort of a work order, always exists in a prayer of petition. The creation of the kingdom is a joint venture between us and God. God is willing, eager to do God's part; we must be willing to do ours.

As a master teacher, Jesus possessed a rich imagination. When he unlocked the mystery of the kingdom for his listeners, he used the wonders of creation with which they were already familiar. He seemed to be particularly interested in seeds, although the Scriptures provide no description of his planting any.

Yet Jesus lived in a semibarren land where food was quite likely in short supply. People knew about growing things. So when Jesus described what the kingdom was like, he asked people to think about the growth of seeds—little seeds growing into great big trees or seeds on hard rocks and rich soil and what happens afterward. Jesus described the kingdom with images of growth— slow, patient growth—that calls for the care and attention of those who did the planting. (That's us, folks!)

When we ask God for the kingdom to come, we might add that the kingdom comes into existence in God's best time, and not ours. We can be impatient sometimes; we ask for a favor, and if it is not done right away, we get discouraged. Yet God seems to do things on a timetable all God's own.

But what we trust and hope and believe in is that the kingdom *is* coming to be. And that's all that matters! God is always supplying the energy and the rest is up to us. "Pray and work" is the ancient motto of the Benedictines, a religious order founded in the sixth century. This is the same pattern we find in the prayer of yearning or asking. We ask God, and then we get to work! Like the old prayer, let us pray as if everything depends on God and act as if everything depends on us!

Prayer and fire

Besides praying for the coming of the kingdom, which is more like a communal prayer, we have another wonderful, more

> *This love will invade them, pervade them, fill them.*

personal prayer in our tradition. This prayer comes from the way we celebrate the Mass on Pentecost and the readings we use when we remember the coming of the Holy Spirit to Jesus' disciples and to us. Teachers often use this prayer, but its meaning goes beyond classroom learning.

> Come, Holy Spirit, fill the hearts of your faithful and enkindle within them the fire of your love.

This is a dangerous prayer. Why? Because it asks God to fire us up, to put within us that passion that is part of God's desires. And if that happens, we will be on fire with love. (But we will also have to be ready!) Remember the rich young man who came to Jesus. He wanted everything, but in order to get it, Jesus said he had to separate himself from worldly possessions for they tended to hold him back from God. The man yearned for something—someone—more; Jesus was quite ready to offer the man what he sought, but the youth appeared not ready to receive Jesus' gift.

We need to note in the story of the rich young man that Jesus didn't respond that the man was asking for too much. Jesus tells us to ask; just go ahead and ask for more and more and more! God can handle our petitions; God likes us to be in touch with our human desires. As was said above, wanting is an important part of our standard equipment. It's where we connect with the real God.

However, there's a catch. We can be so filled up with unimportant stuff (like the rich young man) that we may not have room for God. Even worse, we can forget we are in need. That's why so often the New Testament gives harsh words about the love of money.

Money is power. Lots of money makes one feel more powerful. A whole lot of money can make one feel like God. And that's a big danger. Thus, we encounter one of the important Gospel paradoxes. If we want more, we must have less. If we want to possess everything, we must choose nothing. But if we want to be filled with God's love, with Jesus' love for everyone, then all we need do is ask, and our God will willingly, eagerly, pantingly, fire us up!

Obviously, God does not always give us exactly what we ask for. Rather, God gives us what we truly need. Here, we walk into a deep pool of mystery that we cannot fully know or understand. Within this mystery, God calls forth our trust. Just as in the prayer of acceptance. We trust God and we trust that God knows best. We trust that God knows what's just around the bend!

Like Jesus, we ask for whatever we need or desire. After all, Jesus told us to do this. We ask that God's kingdom come. And immediately after that we pray the next petition of the Our Father: "Your will be done on earth as it is in heaven." We want to receive the best from our prayers—God's best. And God alone knows what that is.

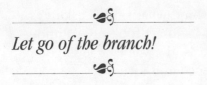

Let go of the branch!

If you had to choose, right now, this minute, that which is *most* important to you and let go of all else (all else!), what would you choose? Your husband or wife? Your kids? Your parent? Your best friend? Perhaps a favorite family memento, such as a piece of heirloom furniture or a photograph taken during the war. Maybe you would choose your home or a family beach home or your job. What or whom would you choose?

We invite you to list (right now) the eight or ten most important things or persons in the world to you. Do not be concerned about the order of your list, just list your choices. Do this before reading the rest of this section.

When you're finished with your list, read on . . .
Now, you must decide to let go of one. Choose one; cross that off your list.

You must now decide to let go of another. Choose one; cross that off your list.

And, again, you must let go of one. Choose one; cross that off your list.

Once more, you must let go. Choose one; cross that off your list.

Again, you must let go of another. Choose one; cross that off your list.

Continue, until you have only one left.

Now, cross that off your list.

Our God invites us to let go of everything and to trust that God knows what we need. However, this is not so much a lesson in actually letting go. (Actually, we will have to do just that someday in order to have what God has prepared for us beyond this life! Rather, letting go is an act of trust and faith in our God.

An old legend may illustrate what God is asking here: Now God never asks us to act foolishly so understand the legend for what it is: the value of letting go and trusting in God's presence and love.

A woman is standing at the edge of a deep gorge. God invites her to jump off the cliff, assuring her that she will fall into the palm of God's hand.

She hesitates, yet encouraged by God's urgings to trust, she does leap forward into the abyss. However, on the way down, she grabs hold of a large branch jutting forth from the mountain side.

Then God says, "You didn't do it yet! Let go of the branch!"

After considerable time and frequent invitations from God, she finally lets go.

Then God says, "You need to let go with the other hand too!"

Someday we, too, will need to let go with both hands. Our God invites us to enter into prayer with God while we are here on this earth. And God invites us to ask for what we want and accept what we need. God asks us to practice letting go and letting God do the rest. God is real good at that.

A Psalm

O God, you are my God, / and I long for you. / My whole being desires you; / like a dry, worn-out, and waterless land, / my soul is thirsty for you./ Let me see you in the sanctuary; / let me see how mighty and glorious you are. / Your constant love is better than life itself, / and so I will praise you. / I will give you thanks as long as I live; / I will raise my hands to you in prayer. / My soul will feast and be satisfied, / and I will sing glad songs of praise to you.

Psalm 63:1–5

You're In for It

Asking is not something we do easily, God.
Especially those of us you created
in the image and likeness of you
Who happen to be the male representation.
We don't even ask for directions,
Or anything else.

We think it's because somehow
We became convinced that we're supposed to solve
the problem
Not depend on somebody else to do it!
And we're really into fixing things, you know.
So asking, depending on anyone,
Is really hard to do.
But we're working on it.
And some of us are making it!

And we would suppose, God,
That you do hear more requests from us
Now that our counterparts are finally welcome
To live more fully
Who they are in the image and likeness of you.

So, in the Spirit of this, God,
We ask that you help us both—
Male and female—
To look to you more to understand us.
Amen.

CHAPTER FIVE

Enjoying Becoming Closer to God

"Bishop this and bishop that . . ." is all he seemed to hear.

His friends had left earlier, but he wanted to hang around awhile. He didn't get away often, and the retreat had been especially good for him this year. As bishop, he cherished any time he could get closer to his God, especially with all he faced every day!

So he hung around and decided to take one more walk on the beautiful grounds before leaving the mountain retreat. He wanted to get in touch with the bit of anxiety he had about leaving. Or perhaps, the anxiety was about going—going back to all the problems: the press, the unending schedule, the tremendous demands on his time over which he no longer had control.

"Bishop this and bishop that . . ." is all he seemed to hear anymore! Moments of true shepherding seemed few and far between. Some days he wished he was just a pastor again. However, on second thought, even that was stressful. Actually, he wished he were back home again with Mom and Dad and Sue and Robert. Those were the days!

"Gosh, we used to have fun," he remembered, as he started down the stone path that went around the grounds. "Such games we played. And mom's food! Nothing like it! Haven't found a housekeeper yet as good as Mom. I need to make her chicken again one of these days. It's been a long time since I did. Maybe Rob and Jean would like to come for a visit. By golly! That's a great idea! I'll throw a reunion! Up at the old family cabin. This summer! And I'll ask everybody to bring stories and recipes! A real 'family' reunion! Back to whatever we can find. Just being us."

Just being us.

The words rang in his own ears. He said them out loud; they brought him to a halt on the pathway. Then he realized he was suddenly eager to go. Now his retreat was complete.

"Thank you, Lord," he said. "You're the best."

> *"On the one hand, in the words of this prayer the only Son gives us the words the Father gave him: he is the master of our prayer. On the other, as Word incarnate, he knows in his human heart the needs of his human brothers and sisters and reveals them to us: he is the model of our prayer."*
>
> CCC, 2765

Six days later Jesus took with him Peter, James, and
John, and led them up a high mountain, where they
were alone. As they looked on, a change came over
Jesus, and his clothes became shining white—whiter
than anyone in the world could wash them. Then the
three disciples saw Elijah and Moses talking with Jesus.
Peter spoke up and said to Jesus, "Teacher, how good
it is that we are here! We will make three tents, one
for you, one for Moses, and one for Elijah." He and the
others were so frightened that he did not know what
to say.

Then a cloud appeared and covered them with its
shadow, and a voice came from the cloud, "This is my
own dear Son—listen to him!" They took a quick look
around but did not see anyone else; only Jesus was with
them. As they came down the mountain, Jesus ordered
them, "Don't tell anyone what you have seen, until the
Son of Man has risen from death."

Mark 9:2–9

_____ ᵉ𝒮

Don't we get "zapped"
once in a while?

ᵉ𝒮
_____

We call this story from the
New Testament Jesus'
transfiguration.
Transfigured, Jesus is
radically changed. Three
of his friends, those who
would need to carry on after his final leaving, witnessed
this transfiguration. We, too, can witness the transformation of Jesus if we but uncover our eyes, pick up our
fear at bay, and turn toward the reality of who Jesus is.

God invites us to take part in Jesus' transfiguration.
How can we do this? By giving our lives over to God to
be transformed. Then we can savor our closeness to
God—until the time of our own resurrection. God invites
us to let go and to reap the joys of transformation.

This is what happened to the man in the opening story of this chapter. He stays on the mountain, awaiting God's final move before leaving his retreat. He lets go. How? By opening himself up—through prayer—to the realization of why he's not ready to leave the mountain. And then God transfigures him by taking him back to home, to family, to his roots. And his life changes. Now he can come down from the mountain for he sees with a new awareness of who and whose he is.

Our lives are like that. Don't we get "zapped" once in a while? Something happens that suddenly sends us in a different direction, transfigures us, so to speak, into the person God deeply desires us to be. Big or little experiences make this happen. We just need to be ready and willing to accept that which happens to us. Then all the goodness within us, (the goodness God knows is within us), finally shines forth for the good of the world around us. And the world is a better place.

> " 'In Christ we have also obtained an inheritance, having been destined according to the purpose of him who accomplishes all things according to his council and will.' We ask insistently for this loving plan to be fully realized on earth as it is already in heaven."
>
> CCC, 2823

> *The pleasures of this life . . . have always found a home in our Catholic tradition.*

Sometimes we have an experience that seems so good we want it to go on forever. Perhaps we saw a movie that brought us into a world of full enjoyment. Or maybe we were with someone very special from our family or with a best friend and while we were together, life seemed wonderful. In those moments, the prayer in our heart is "O God. Please don't let this end."

We hope that everyone has special moments when life is great. When might this happen? When we come to a reunion of people who were close once, drifted apart, and then came back together; when we watch our child achieve or excel in some venture; when the sky seems so incredible and the air smells so sweet, that we feel as if creation has begun again and we are the first to see its beauty. In those moments, we rejoice in life. And we should, because God calls us to enjoy life.

Over the centuries some Christians went down a terribly wrong road. They assumed that life was meant to be hard and burdensome; they thought that having fun was something created more by the devil than by God. They boycotted parties; they felt that laughing or smiling was wrong; they blessed seriousness and condemned revelry. They believed in happiness, but not on this earth and not in this life. Earth was for work; play came later, much later! Actually, in the next life!

Generally speaking the Catholic Church has not fallen victim to this sour interpretation of life. The pleasures of this life, whether they come from social life or from the life of the mind, have always found a home in our Catholic tradition. Catholics can be very serious at times, but we don't take this to extremes—at least, as a part of our faith.

Praise and play

We do not need sour and serious faces.

٭

The word *praise* is a very common religious word. Many hymns and psalms call us to "praise God." But what is this act of praise?

If our idea of God imagines God as distant, impersonal, or ambivalent, then praise may mean falling down in obedience to the power over life and death. With this view of God, we praise with words like "God is great and wonderful; we are nothing but horrible sinners." This attitude can lead us to see a great distance between God and ourselves.

Imagine that the president of our country had lived next door to us early in life. If this were true, any letter we wrote to the president would be full of familiar references and informal asides. We would probably use the president's first name or even a nickname.

Contrast that kind of letter with one we would write if we didn't know the president and if we grew up in a family in which authority was always threatening. If we were from that kind of background, we would probably be formal and distant.

Now which approach—friendly or distant—fits with the spirit of our religious faith? God has invited us to be friends. God invites us to be family. God's intent in creating us is to bring us closer. In fact, God wants us to relate to God on a first-name basis.

Jesus taught us how to use "Abba" when praying. Thus, we address God as loving parent. God is not stern, inflexible, dominating, authoritarian. No. God is loving. God is the one who loves to be with us just as a parent loves to visit with us or rejoice with us or laugh to the point of collapse with us.

So we do not need sour and serious faces when we pray! In fact, smiling might just delight God. We can be

sure that God smiles at us when we share happiness!
And God cries with us when we share sorrows.

Fancy words, big words, or "churchy" words aren't
necessary either. Ordinary conversational language is
okay when we talk to God. After all, we think in
ordinary language and God knows our every thought.
We use this language when we share our lives with our
best friends. And God is one of those!

Does this sound disrespectful? Not to the God who
enjoys a walk in the coolness of the evening. The God
who is always with us and _____
for us and by us and *How blessed we are*
around us and above us
and below us and within *if we can play.*
us. This God who feels our _____
feelings and knows every breath we take. Not to this
God who is as close to us as the beat of our own heart.

The words *play* and *pray* are very similar; so is their
meaning. To play is to let the particular experience of
the moment fill us so fully that there is scarcely room
for any other thoughts. Play takes energy, yet it rejuve-
nates us and gives us more energy. Those of us who
know how to play, how to be fully present and deeply
aware of joy, are able to savor life.

How blessed we are if we can play! If we can enjoy
being together as family or friends, just sitting around the
table and wasting time with each other. How blessed we
are if we can let go of lists and "have-to's" that can wait
and if we can pour our energy into making memories!

The prayer of enjoyment is the kind of prayer that
affirms God and all God wants for us. It's the "Yea
God!" prayer. It's an "Alleluia!" that comes from the
depths of our heart. And just as during the Easter season
(when the Alleluia is usually said twice), so, too, our
sense of life is expanded when we pray with joy. Then
one "Alleluia!" just isn't enough!

Enjoyment and simple gratitude

We are not human doings; we are human beings!

The bishop in our opening story has just spent many days reflecting on his life, his role in the church, and his responsibilities. But what excites him at this moment? What energizes him? Family. His growing up. The good times. The memories. The fun. The play. And he wonders whether he can create more.

Let's note that when the bishop begins to imagine a family reunion, he does not think about how wonderful it will be for the family to have the family bishop around. Nor does he imagine simply going back to an earlier time when things were better or simpler. No, one thought excites him—just being together.

God has given us life, and it's not just for the future, it's happening right now! Someone once said, "Life is what happens while we're making other plans." Is life passing us by? How can we avoid this? If we are open to possibilities, life becomes a wonderful adventure to enjoy and live to its fullest right now. And life can be this way when we become aware of our God's presence. Thus, we pray out of our joy and we reflect on God, the beginning and the end and the in fact, the cause of our joy.

To allow our joy and our God to enter our awareness, sometimes we need to let go of so much busyness. We need to slow down for a few moments and find the deep center of ourselves where God, our joy, dwells. Moments of simple pleasure and simple prayer.

We are not human doings; we are human beings! When we allow ourselves to be the wonderful creations God called into being, then we always find room for joy. God created us, first of all, to enjoy our life, to party!

What can we do to give families the freedom to be about their holy family business?

Living day in and day out without much happening that we enjoy is fairly easy. In fact, we're probably following the schedules everybody else sets for us! We've said this before in this familystyle catechism, but think about it again for a minute.

Other people, institutions, and organizations pretty much plan our lives. (This includes places such as the workplace, schools, athletics, medical care, and even churches!) These groups started out to serve our family, to help our family do its holy work. Then something happened and the groups started to take over many of the responsibilities and rights of our family, which is the primary community of life and love.

For example, our jobs tell us when to leave family and when to return. Our employers are frequently more understanding of a broken-down car than a broken-down child or other family member. In fact, we often have to lie about taking time to be with family members when they need us.

Moreover, we parents feel guilty when we have to leave work to take care of family business. So many other institutions (like those in the medical field) are available to us only during work hours. So we feel the crunch in our lives to fit into schedules.

Most schools and other educational places, like community centers, retreat centers, parishes, and so on, also lack a family sensitivity. They plan for the individual and not for the entire system, although the entire family is affected when children have to be at school at the same time a parent has to be across town at work! Or when a child has to be at religious education class early on Saturday morning and that's the only day the family has to relax and enjoy it's own holy experience of one another!

These institutions are not sensitive to family when they schedule opportunities for adult learning only at times when people with children have to be home with them. If institutions want to strengthen families, they need to walk in our shoes and plan with us in mind. What do they need to change so that they can help our family as a whole? What can they do to help support the holy work of our family?

Those of us who do the planning for these institutions are family members too, even if we are not married or parents. All of us belong to family. The planners—the educators, the coaches, the bosses, the coworkers, the volunteer leader, the catechist, the store manager—aren't isolated bad persons who rule our lives. They are us! Family people. Human beings with some of the same needs and wants. Especially the need to simply be family; to build up holy memories; to enjoy one another and the relaxation, joy, and laughter our God intended.

What can we do to help families be less stressed? What can we do to give them the freedom to be about their holy family business? How can we really value the enjoyable moments in our life, especially those in family? We need to think about these questions, and we need to find our answers in prayerful meditation and conversation with others who are affected by our decisions.

A Psalm

Give thanks to the Lord with harps,
sing to him with stringed instruments.
Sing a new song to him,
play the harp with skill, and shout for joy!

We put our hope in the Lord;
he is our protector and our help.
We are glad because of him;
we trust in his holy name.
May your constant love be with us, Lord,
as we put our hope in you.

Psalm 33:2–3, 20–22

God's Playground

emember the playground
In your old neighborhood,
Or maybe in your imagination,
Where everything a kid might want
was there?
Including no Mom saying, "It's time to come home."

Where do these ideas come from, these fantasies
That dance in our minds,
So wonderful, so exciting?

Well, what do you think?
They came from the great player in heaven—
God—who lives in the grandest playground of all
And longs for the day
When we can all come to play
And hear the smiling voice of God say,
"Come play with me
And all the rest,
I've made it all for you,
And you deserve the very best."

CHAPTER SIX

Re-MEMBER-ing—The Prayer of Jesus and Family

In their American home was an altar, just as there was one in Vietnam.

Many, many years had passed since Saigon fell. Yet Ahn and Le never forgot, nor did thousands of others. And they continued to tell the stories to the children who were too small to remember. And now, to the children's children. The stories of torture, of fear, of horror, of pain. And the stories of escape.

Part of *this* family's story was of life since coming to the United States, no matter why or how they got here. Like the first immigrants to this land of promise, Ahn's family had lived enough life here to have the stories of pain lessen and the stories of new struggles and joys replace them. But she and Le never forgot.

They always thought about the six children they had to leave behind. In spite of the fact they'd had other children since coming, the first family—the one Ahn's parents finished raising—were always their family too.

Today was a day they'd waited for ever since they left. One of their *first* children had gotten out. She was coming with friends to find them.

In their American home was an altar, just as there had been one in Vietnam. They'd kept the custom for it was good. And they prayed at their altar frequently.

Ahn found herself there today, kneeling in the bedroom in front of the little shelf, looking up toward the statue. Emotion overwhelmed her heart. Never, ever had she imagined that she'd see any of these babies again. She felt such joy, tempered only by the sadness of the memories of the other five children she'd had to leave behind.

Her tears began to fall. She looked up at the Sacred Heart statue. Emotion coursed through her whole being, and she began to pray.

"Our Father, who art in heaven . . ."

And Ahn felt God gently holding *her* heart.

"The 'our' at the beginning of the Lord's Prayer, like the 'us' of the last four petitions, excludes no one. If we are to say it truthfully, our divisions and oppositions have to be overcome."

CCC, 2792

"When you pray, do not use a lot of meaningless words,
as the pagans do, who think that their gods will hear
them because their prayers are long. Do not be like
them. Your Father already knows what you need before
you ask him. This, then, is how you should pray:
'Our Father in heaven:
May your holy name be honored;
may your Kingdom come;
may your will be done on earth as it is in heaven.
Give us today the food we need.
Forgive us the wrongs we have done,
as we forgive the wrongs that others have done to us.
Do not bring us to hard testing,
but keep us safe from the Evil One.' "

Matthew 6: 7–13

*The point is, Jesus chose
family relationships.*

This is pretty clear, isn't it?
Jesus is telling us not to
ramble on and on
because God already
knows our hearts. All we
need do is open up the
door; state our connection in family words ("father");
then, continuing, ask simply for the *kingdom* right here,
right now (". . . thy kingdom come . . ."). Of course,
we also need our *food* today (" . . . give us this day . . .")
to nourish our bodies, our minds, and our lives.

Then, in our partnership with God, we need to *forgive*
(". . . forgive us our trespasses as we forgive . . .").
That is, we must forgive—no ifs, ands, or buts about
this forgiving. We have to do it! People will treat us the
way we treat them. So in order to be forgiven for our
wrongdoing to others, we must make the first move and
forgive others. This is absolutely necessary if we are to
love as God loves and if we are to follow the example
of Jesus.

One wonderful reality of the Lord's Prayer is that it fits so well into the arena of family. A lot of the terminology within it is home language: *Father, name, obey, food, forgive, others, safe.* Great family language! Of course, we could guess why Jesus did this because he hung out in families! All forms of families. (Let's remember here that Jesus was from a nontraditional family, the foster son of Joseph.)

Also, Jesus used family language—*father, son*—to describe our relationship to God. He could have used *mother* and *daughter* or *grandfather* and *grandchild* or other family roles. The point is, Jesus chose *family* relationships.

Even here, in the way we connect with God through prayer, we find family stuff. Sort of a re-MEMBER-ing, a recalling of the memories of family and a *reconnecting* the MEMBERS of family.

This is true for the woman in our opening story. She is comfortable with praying the Our Father in the sanctuary of her home, the holy place in which she and her husband and children struggle with life. She uses her special altar with its statue to help herself pray, to help herself concentrate on her God.

Yet, her home and the reality of her family, not the statue on the altar, are the focus of her prayer. Within her family, she turns to God in thanksgiving, as she re-MEMBERS (once again) her first children.

> *"God's care for all . . . should extend our prayer to the full breadth of love whenever we dare to say 'our' Father."*
>
> CCC, 2793

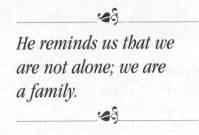

He reminds us that we are not alone; we are a family.

"Where is he?" one of the close followers of Jesus asked.

"He's over there. Down by the water. He's probably praying. He's been doing a lot of that lately."

His followers knew Jesus as a person of prayer. Sometimes he prayed at night, sometimes in the morning. He never missed a day. Some of the apostles felt that the time had come to ask him about prayer. For a long time now, they had known that he liked questions. Everyone, friend and foe, asked Jesus questions, as if to test him. And everyone also knew that he gave interesting, provocative, unpredictable answers. He made them think. So, they must have decided, let's question him about prayer!

According to the Gospel of Luke, the disciples asked Jesus about prayer one day after he had himself finished praying. In his response, Jesus did not give them a prayer, but rather, he shared with them a way to pray. He wanted them to remember to pray in the spirit of the prayer we call the Our Father.

Praying like this changes us because it reminds us who we are. The act itself brings forth special awarenesses, in us. For instance, in the Our Father Jesus begins by addressing _our_ father. He reminds us that we are not alone; we are a family. We are a family connected with everyone. And so, when we speak as a family member or pray as a family member, we start with a sense of _us_ as in the traditional invitation, _"Let us pray."_

Another awareness that Jesus helps us develop is the spirit of approaching God as our divine _parent_. When we pray to God, we are reminded that our very life comes from God. We are related to this God as child to loving parent—father and mother.

Remembering and awareness

Jesus reminds us there are no outsiders.

We have entitled this chapter re-MEMBER-ing. The word *remember* has two important meanings. First, we draw from our memory those events and people of our history that we want to keep as part of our present life. Our memory pulls the past into the present; it expands our sense of what's right here and now. With our memories we even bring back the dead when we look at old family photos. With our memories we think about the past and move more deeply into our awareness of the present.

The Our Father connects us with all who have gone before us into God's love and with all who still live here on earth. We call on the God of all of us—the living and the dead. Thus, the Our Father connects us to all we can remember, because all—the people we have loved, the experiences we have had, the dreams we have dreamed—live on in God. In this prayer, we remember our life as members of a family.

Second, prayer can help us actually connect with other members of God's family, those we love and even those we don't. Prayer connects us to others.

From a Christian standpoint, prayer can even connect us with our enemies. In the Our Father we pray that others will forgive us as we forgive them. The others are those who have done us wrong. We could easily list them as outsiders, but in his prayer, Jesus reminds us that in the kingdom there are no outsiders. We are all one—just as Jesus prayed that we all be one as he and his father are one.

Our family prayer

The Our Father is the family prayer of the church! It uses family language and relates to typical family events like dinner time, forgiveness time, don't-stay-out-too-late-lest-you-be-led-into-temptation time.

When an individual member of our family prays, our whole family, in a sense, prays. Family connections are there even though we don't think about them. But how much better to think about each other and to pray for each other! Just praying for another person brings us closer.

Scientists have estimated that each of us receives two or three thousand messages each day. (By messages they mean everything we are aware of—from something said to us by a friend to our senses picking up a change in the weather.) We are like giant radio receivers pulling all kinds of messages from the sky; news is always coming in.

Change in family is always happening.

Once we receive the message, we respond. How? We ignore some messages; others we judge to be important and we do something about them. And all this changes us, because we cannot take something into ourselves without being changed in the process. Our "conversation" with our environment changes us; the outside comes inside and the inside changes.

Even when we are separated from family members for a relatively short period of time, we may notice change in them. If we extend this separation over many weeks, months, or years, we will note a lot of change. Change in family is always happening, and change sometimes hurts. All of us—parents, spouses, children—know this. In truth, children often end up being the tragic victims of the changes in other family members.

That's one of the reasons why we pray about forgiveness.

Jesus prayed that we would be one in spirit, one in truth. In our prayer with and for others, we draw upon the power of God to pull us together, as God intended in the first place. That's family.

Let's think for a moment about remembering. God formed our family from the beginning of time; over centuries, our ancestors formed us through countless kind and supportive gestures and big and little dreams and helpful and careful actions. And some of this formation came through their sins and through our own unkind and hurtful actions. When we pray, we remember all those who have gone before and who have prayed *our* Father. We—family—are all in this together!

". . . the presence of those who hunger because they lack bread opens up another profound meaning . . . The drama of hunger in the world calls Christians who pray sincerely to exercise responsibility . . . both in their personal behavior and in their solidarity with the human family."

CCC, 2831

Like artists, we create a unique masterpiece— ourselves.

Prayer can change us, if we are open to change. In truth, God doesn't need our prayer, but we need to pray because it allows us to weave together all the separate pieces of ourselves and our life. Prayer helps us see the patterns in our lives, some of which are destructive, some of which are wholesome. And prayers helps us make choices about what we will do with these patterns. Like artists, we take all the different parts of our life and, with God's help, create a unique master-piece—ourselves! Just as God intended! Thus, we change.

The Lord's Prayer, said with imagination, connects us with some of the family parts of our life.

For instance, we can paraphrase Jesus' prayer more specifically to family by saying and thinking the following:

"Our Father" . . . and our mother, and all who give us life, even strange Uncle Bob . . .

"who art in heaven" . . . and although you may be 'up there' you are also 'down here' in the noisy and quiet times of our life and in the things we see that are you in our kids.

"hallowed be your name" . . . meaning holy, ordinary holiness, getting really involved in life, caring about others, so when we make your name holy, you do the same for us . . .

"thy kingdom come" . . . in other words, YES! Make good happen all over the place (especially on Saturday morning in our home) . . .

"thy will be done on earth as it is in heaven" . . . the way it is "up there" we want "down here," too, and since there's a lot of loving up there, let's have more of that here! . . .

"Give us this day our daily bread" . . . We can always use more bread as in your body for us, but we can also use bread for those kids who go to bed hungry . . .

"and forgive us our trespasses as we forgive those who trespass against us" . . . the hard words! Yes, we will forgive all the misunderstandings and accidental or intentional times we stepped on each other's feet and even the terrible times; the almost unforgivable times; all of it—not so that you forgive us, but because we really do forgive others! And you just happen to do the same for us!

"and lead us not into temptation" . . . and there are plenty of those temptations, like letting others do the dirty work around the house, like not saying we're sorry because we can't face those who are close to us, and like facing decisions—hundreds of times!—about doing right or wrong.

"but deliver us from evil" . . . like the evil involved in pulling away from each other or like the evil we allow to come into our homes via the television set.

"Amen" . . . Yes! . . . we say "Yes!" to everything that builds us as a family, the hard and difficult, the joyful and the playful, everything, that we face every day of our lives!

A Psalm

Praise God . . . / Praise God's strength in heaven! / Praise God for the mighty things God has done. / Praise God's supreme greatness. / Praise God with trumpets. / Praise God with harps and lyres. / Praise God with drums and dancing. / Praise God with harps and flutes. / Praise God with cymbals. / Praise him with loud cymbals. / Praise the Lord, all living creatures! *From Psalm 150*

Make a Lot of Noise!

hank God we finally know
That prayer also means
That it's okay for us to praise God
With cymbals, LOUD cymbals!

Because that also means God expects
Babies to cry
And cry out loud!
And children to yell for Mommy
Or Daddy or Gramma or Grandpa
So all the world can hear
We belong!
There's family around here somewhere!
In a hundred different ways
Families let it be known
Hear us!
Pay attention!
We're alive, we're praising God
Doing what God wanted in the first place—
Loving each other
Through the daily messiness of being family.

And yes,
Sometimes we even yell at one another
To clear God's air.
And then we get back to the stuff of forgiving
And being forgiven.

Thank goodness the word's out
That God who is in heaven,
Understands what it means
To be a parent or family, right here on earth!